DAVID,
Thanks so
much for
all your support.

Milo Watson

73

What the Night Demands
a collection of poetry

ങ

by Miles Walser

Write Bloody Publishing
America's Independent Press

Austin, TX

WRITEBLOODY.COM

Walser, Miles.
1ˢᵗ edition.
ISBN: 978-1938912-16-0

Interior Layout by Lea C. Deschenes
Cover Art & Illustration by Lily Lin
Author Photo by Rosemary Spolar
Proofread by Sean Patrick Mulroy & Helen Novelli
Edited by Derrick C. Brown, Megan Falley & Sean Patrick Mulroy
Type set in Bergamo from www.theleagueofmoveabletype.com

Printed in Tennessee, USA

Write Bloody Publishing
Austin, TX
Support Independent Presses
writebloody.com

To contact the author, send an email to writebloody@gmail.com

MADE IN THE USA

For Mateo, my oldest friend.
You are where this book began.

And for Megan.
Love, you make everything feel possible.

WHAT THE NIGHT DEMANDS

"This night demands much of all of us. And the days that follow will demand even more."

—Norwegian Prime Minister Jens Stoltenberg
July 22, 2011

What the Night Demands

I.

Definitions from the Practical American Dictionary 19

Bang 20

Grace 22

Hierarchy of Trans-Ness at the High School Queer Youth Mixer ... 24

An Apology to My Sisters 26

A Triptych of Anxiety 27

Introverted Me and Lonely Me on a Couch at a Party 30

The Roommate 31

Nebraska 32

Sideshow 33

The Perfectionist's Head Cold 34

II.

Ex-Boyfriend Me Mocks Boyfriend Me from across Campus 39

The First Day of Spring 40

We Eat an Apple in My Bed 41

Lost Boys 42

Inheritance 43

Bitch 44

Birthday Girl 45

Thoughtful Me Runs into Asshole Me at the Bank 46

Lamprocapnos Spectabilis 47

Waiting 48

Photograph: My First Day of Preschool 49

Acrostic for Cleveland 50

Madison, Wisconsin 51

White Me Talks to an Empty Room About His Skin 52

III.

Seven-Year-Old Me Takes Seventy-Year-Old Me
to the Playground 57

Anna 58

Oxford Comma the Cat Talks Back 59

Christina 61

The Writer 62

On Loving a Survivor 63

Letter to My Vagina 64

First Shower 65

August 66

Biology 67

The Man I Am Tries to Take the Girl
I Was through Airport Security 68

While Getting My Blood Drawn at the Trans Health Clinic 69

I.

DEFINITIONS FROM THE PRACTICAL AMERICAN DICTIONARY

Man (v):

- *To take. To build. To destroy. To love so hard you can't open your fists.*

- *To be. To be right. To be worthy. To be the reason the buddy system exists.*

- *To own. To own everything. To own yourself.*

- *To feel powerful. To not understand your power until a weaker thing tries to take some of it for themselves.*

- *To make mistakes without shame. e.g. To fasten a volume knob to everything pretty and hide the remote control.*
  To have control sitting in your pocket, resting against your thigh. To think control rests against your thigh.

- *To walk alone. To sleep with unlocked windows. To breathe deep, without worry.*

woman (adj):

- *to be defined by faults, e.g. a cavity waiting to be filled.*

- *pliable, easy to break e.g. an ice cream cone smashed by a greedy grip.*

- *helpless, especially without a set of instructions or owner. e.g. a fly trapped under a glass jar.*

BANG

I learned how to talk about sex in my high school hallway,
the locker room after gym, a dirty secret—
gum stuck beneath a desk, a word etched in a bathroom stall.

Sex was the ubiquitous celebrity—
the rock star with so many monikers, you never knew what to call it.
Teachers mumbled *Intercourse*,
mothers whispered *Making Love*,
but we stripped the training wheels from our own bikes
and dared each other across traffic.

Fuck. Nail. Bang.

Sex is pressing your ear to the seashell of someone's body,
holding the hum of crest and crash.
The way we speak massacres it
into the business of shoplifted skin.

Hit that. Get some. Take it.

There are times when I am unsure if I am listening to a story
about a night with a lover or a back-alley fistfight.

Pin. Pound. Screw.

We run through other people's homes
with muddy feet and baseball bats
Grind. Smash. swinging at anything beautiful
Get a piece. but we're surprised
when something shatters.
Jump her bones.

The first time you force your lover down,
you will only be listening to instructions.
Won't understand softness, that an arching back
should not snap into splinters.
We are told names are as harmless
as a playground bully, a dull blade,

but you won't know how to bloom your fist into an open palm.
You will not hear the No.

Call something the same name a few times,
it will begin to answer to it.
Fuck. Nail. Bang.
Bang.
Bang.

GRACE

Grace, you're four years old?
Grace, that's old!
Grace, look at that sunflower. Isn't it pretty?
Grace, you have Cinderella at your house?
Grace, pizza is my favorite too.
Grace, what's the first letter of your name?
Grace, even princesses have to raise their hand.
Grace, even princesses have to stand in line.
Grace, yes, I've heard of Justin Beaver.
Grace, my name's not Teacher.
Grace, I'm Miles. My name is Miles.
Grace, does it matter if I'm a boy or girl?
Grace, don't pull my hair.
Grace, I don't have girl hair.
Grace, no, my hair isn't broken.
Grace, yes, you can trace my tattoos with crayons.
Grace, what makes you think there are boy clothes and girl clothes?
Grace, what makes a color a girl color?
Grace, you can't put me in jail.
Grace, no, I'm not married.
Grace, yes, maybe someday I'll get married.
Grace, no, I don't have a girlfriend.
Grace, no, I can't *buy* a girlfriend.
Grace, these aren't girl sandals. I just have sandals.
Grace, use your words.
Grace, not those words.
Grace, yes, I'll read you a book.
Grace, no, not ten books.
Grace, don't pull my shirt like that.
Grace, it's not a girl shirt.
Grace, where should your hands be right now?
Grace, never run toward a busy street.
Grace, because it scares me.
Grace, I don't have a girl mouth. It's just a mouth.
Grace, is now a talking time?
Grace, I need you to be quiet, your friends are sleeping.

Grace, I'm not a girl.
Grace, can you please listen?
Grace, I need you to listen.
Grace, should you talk to your friends like that?
Grace, you can play after your time out.
Grace, you're hurting my feelings.
Grace, I'm not a girl.
Grace, that's not funny.
Grace, No, because boys don't wear dresses.

Miles, what makes you think there are boy clothes and girl clothes?
Miles, was that the right thing to say?
Miles, where should your hands be right now?
Miles, never run towards a busy street.
Miles, I need you to listen.
Miles, because it scares me.
Miles, use your words.
Miles, not those words.

Hierarchy of Trans-Ness at the High School Queer Youth Mixer

I. Machismo, the Trans Prince

When I enter the room,
everything feminine faints in my presence.
I am a contagious plague of sexy.
Every face snaps towards me like a school
of starving fish praying to be reeled in.

I roll with a gang ready to shin-kick
the first person who dares not call me Mister.
I am a gender-bending James Dean—
my hair an impenetrable coat of cool.
Every other butch thing wishes they were me.
I'm so butch they call it courage.

I strut manly *and* sensitive—
a football team that hugs it out
and sings acoustic versions of 90s alt-rock love songs.

I am the coolest oppressed kid in the room—
my oppression out-oppresses all the normal gay boys.
My gay boy friends are bathroom bouncers,
guarding the men's room door while I pee.

Every cup of punch I drink is spiked with
"Tonight is MY night, motherfucker!"
The DJ plays all my requests. I ask any girl to dance.
The room is bowing to me—
they're calling me their King.

II. Amanda, the Easy Target

She has not been asked to dance all night.
Nobody is complimenting her dress—
we all just stare, waiting for an outline
of stuffing. It's impossible to divorce
the shape of her body from her new name,
so we don't even try.

She's at her third school this year—
the teasing, the graffiti on her locker
is painted all over her.

Tonight she talks to the chaperones,
holds hands with her glass of punch.
In the next year she'll probably win
a death threat, a nudge
towards the edge of a building,
the knot in her noose.

In November, we will both celebrate
Transgender Day of Remembrance.
We'll pretend we've lost the same things.

AN APOLOGY TO MY SISTERS
after Jeanann Verlee

I'm sorry I was born first. I'm sorry the hand-me-down shirts billowed around you. Sorry I bossed you around. Made you clean my room. Pushed you out the front door. Sorry I cut our hair. I'm sorry I was held up to you like a mirror. I'm sorry I refused to take ballet. Sorry I insisted on baseball. I'm sorry I wasn't a faster runner. I'm sorry you could always catch up. I'm sorry I wouldn't let you play with my friends. I'm sorry I locked my door. Wouldn't let you climb into my bed. I'm sorry I cursed at Mom. Cursed at Dad. Cursed at you. I'm sorry I started hiding my name in coughs. Sorry I stopped playing princess. I'm sorry I was an empty stoop after a ditched doorbell. I'm sorry you borrowed my clothes. I'm sorry there were no dresses left in my closet. I'm sorry I let you go to school dressed like *that*. Like me. I'm sorry the other girls laughed. I should have bought mascara you could steal. I'm sorry I was the wrong guidebook. The wrong language. I'm sorry I was a dirty joke you'd never tell a grown-up. I'm sorry I wore a tuxedo to prom. I was a bad teacher. I'm sorry I disappeared. I'm sorry I wouldn't let you follow. I'm sorry I'm in all your photo albums. It's okay, cut me out. I'm sorry I was a sister. Who didn't stay a sister.

A TRIPTYCH OF ANXIETY

I. Praise to the Internet!

O brilliant back-lit best friend! Better
than sunlight warming closed eyelids.
Better than direct eye contact.

O cartoon villain! Popping up
next to my deadlines with a new joke,
a story I need to hear now!
My playmate that never grows tired.

O wingman! Always ready
to lend a hand when I am convinced
I am not lonely enough.
When it's easier to imagine
entering strange, nameless women.

 O secret teacher! Answering
my test questions through
an invisible earpiece. I ask you everything
I won't admit to not already knowing.

II. The Artful Dodge

I can't, too tired.
     I've had a long day at work.
     I should really get some writing done.
     [then just smile and shrug your shoulders].
     I need to go to bed early.
     I have a big day tomorrow.
     I shouldn't spend the money.
     I just ate dinner.
     I had a cold last week and should take it slow.
     the busses stop running at midnight.
     too far to bike.
     I've never been there before.
     I don't already have the menu memorized.
     I eat when I'm nervous.
     turns out I'm not funny.
     I look boring in everything I own.
     girls don't find me charming.
     once I said yes and regretted it.
     I may swerve my bike towards traffic.
     this chair is the only thing I can manage right now.
     I want to,
     but I can't.

III. Lies I've Told my Therapists, in Reverse Chronological Order

On my days off I leave my apartment
explore the city or grab coffee with a friend.
The grocery stores here don't make my hands sweat.
I haven't had the urge since I moved.
I know who to call if I'm feeling sad.
No, I haven't even thought of it.
I hurt myself once in high school, but not since.

I have enough money to make it.
I'm not nervous about moving.
Yes, I ate dinner.

I run five miles because I like it.
I only hurt myself the one time
in middle school, but that's it.
No, sex never scares me.

I can tell my mom anything.
I don't really feel sad, I guess.
I don't care.
I don't *need* her.
I never fight with my girlfriend.

Yeah, I must've been.
It was kind of an accident.
Everyone in seventh grade.
I'm friends with everyone.

I know what that means.
No, I didn't read that in a book.
I like having two bedrooms cause I have lots of toys.
Yes, I understand why I'm here.

INTRODUCED ME AND LONELY ME ON A COUCH AT A PARTY

He wants to swallow the room:
every pulsing, beer-soaked inch of it.

This is just like being trapped
inside an auditorium filled with fireworks—how awful

to be denied a whisper. He asks, *Can't we go
lick a quarter from behind that brunette girl's ear?*

A stranger spills next to us on the couch.
He elbows me to introduce myself, gawking

at a group of boys tossing balls into cups of beer—
memorizing every rule in case I ever let him play.

The girl with breath like melting sugar sits down in our lap—
I am gluing my eyelashes to the television.

I am spending our Friday night playing witness
to this imperfect celebration of nothing.

He is undressing
the label on my unfinished drink.

THE ROOMMATE

When we moved in, we were amazed at how big our apartment felt—
had no idea we could fit
- A revolving door of your friends
- A cacophony of radios and dial tones
- The doctors praising me for doing everything right
- Three EMTs
- The same directions to the hospital, scratching again and again from my throat
- The to-do list pinned to my hands to stop the shaking
- Three police officers
- The heaviest phone call to your mother
- Your sister thanking me for saving your life
- My parents advising me that moving out might feel safer
- A scrapbook of goodbyes, each unfinished
- Your notebook, a crimson stain purposefully smeared across it
- The next morning's daylight smashing through our window
- The soapsuds and blood circling the drain as I cleaned off your kitchen knife
- The vacuum trying to suck the night out of the carpet

NEBRASKA

for Brandon Teena

You buried your tampons
under mattresses, cut your hair short, hid
your voice in the deepest part of your chest,
caged yourself under an ace bandage. For years.

You shuffled around gas stations,
never looked men in the eyes.

We share unwanted wombs.
While mine collects cobwebs,
yours lies in a coffin in Nebraska—
the state that made you
famous. Movie script unrolled
from your death certificate.
Your murder, Oscar-worthy.

We are walking obituaries.
Your hate crime headline already carved
across my forehead. People stare at me
and see your delicate hands, point
to where an Adam's Apple should be.

The movie screen is a mirror.
I watch them push you
to the dirt and drag me
into their car, drive a wrench
between your thighs, tear
themselves through my body.

We aren't real men to them.

They won't remember our names
until they read them on our tombstones.
Will decide you are better off splattered
ink on newspaper. They will use you
as a warning for the rest of us.

There are days where it works.

SIDESHOW

"I teach your poems, and when students ask me if you are a boy or a girl, I tell them, 'she can be whatever you want her to be.'"
—*Person who approached me after a poetry show*

How my mother's breast milk must have spoiled.

I am a rigged game at the carnival—
an oval hoop for a spherical ball,
the goldfish guaranteed
to die in your glass bowl.

I am two fists,
held behind your back,
each option
empty.

THE PERFECTIONIST'S HEAD COLD

He is careful to never cry,
or drool, or make a mess,
but today he can't stop his face from spilling
into every tissue in the house.
Nose red as correcting ink,
slipping off onto his cheeks, sloppy.
When he coughs up tea, he is convinced
recovery is reserved for someone strong.
His twenty-four hour bug mutates
into an army of gnawing termites.
He is an oak tree too stupid to fend them off.
Bed rest is being asked to lay still
with the person he trusts the least.
The cold will push into his brain—
whatever is left of it—and mismatch his neurons
until he ties his hair and combs his shoelaces.
He will be scrapped for parts—
his faulty organs lined up like a junkyard.
Staring into his reflection, dry and flaking, he wonders
if, like a snake, he might shed his skin for something tougher.
Or if he will always feel the same
and it will never be well enough.

II.

EX-BOYFRIEND ME MOCKS BOYFRIEND ME FROM ACROSS CAMPUS

Quit ignoring me. Coward. You think you can handpick memory like a bouquet of flowers, pluck amnesia petals each time you meet a new woman. As if tipping over from love means you were never shoved out a front door. When you look at tulips, do you not see the kitchen of your first love? Isn't the one you never wanted waiting for you on every train? When I show up, wearing a familiar name, you swat me away, as if I were trying to ruin your new love. I want nothing from her—I am the shirt the last one gave you. If you are lucky, you can tuck me neatly into a drawer and you will never think of me. Or wear me so often you forget where I came from. But when you feel the ache of a fight, I return, the first step towards the edge of a station platform. You are not unforgettable. She makes you feel like the only working bulb in a city of broken lights. I remind you how easy it is to be replaced.

THE FIRST DAY OF SPRING

That afternoon, sexual health advocates on campus
slipped us a goodie bag of condoms,
marveled at our fingers interlaced
as if we were cradling all the love we'd made.

Back home she laughed, threw the still-wrapped bag
into the garbage as she undressed me
down to my sterile body, the best parts plastic.

It's lucky we don't have to worry, she said,
I almost don't believe you're real.

WE EAT AN APPLE IN MY BED

We've been kissing for months. Three times a week our toothbrushes share a chipped porcelain mug in my bathroom. As my lips reach for the juice falling from her laugh, her mom calls. I listen as she talks about Biology, her new job, asks about her sister. Her eyes drop as she whispers, *No, I still don't have a boyfriend.*

On cue, I stop chewing. She looks at me, waiting for my face to flush, for me to tear from the bed, but I won't get mad at her. She shouldn't have to explain why we can't go swimming in public, why I don't own a razor, why she doesn't need to buy birth control. She hangs up the phone; I pick up the fruit, tell her *Apparently, there's a tiny amount of cyanide in apple seeds.*

She shrugs, says she can handle a little danger, but I've studied how her dimples disappear when she lies, and I know she's thinking about a man she could parade around her family, who could kiss her scratchy with stubble. The kind of man I'll never be.

She squeezes my hand in the movie theater dark but tosses it to the side in front of her friends. Says she just needs time. She walks on the sidewalk. I walk in the street. She closes the door. I kiss it goodnight. She goes home for Thanksgiving. I promise not to call.

If I were a postcard, she could hide me in her pocket. If I were clay, she could mold my body into something easier to love. If I were the guy who sells her a cup of coffee every morning, I could smile at her anonymously, safe as a stranger.

She kisses down my neck, my peel hiding the rotten fruit inside me. As I tell her about the cyanide, her head resting on my chest, she talks about cider, autumn pies. *See*, she says, *Apples are harmless.* But she saves the last bites for me, scared to let her lips wander too close to the core.

Lost Boys

It was the summer you taught me how to pee in public,
how to fight a car windshield, how to bulldoze
through a crowd and not spill a sip.
I learned to hide in your echo.

It was the summer I started confusing sadness
for hunger, worry
for hunger.

It was the summer of too much. Too much
dirty rap music from the dangling speakers
hanging themselves out your bedroom window.

The only way I could say *I love you*
was to keep bandages near the front door.
The only way I could say *I'm scared for us both*
was to eat a whole pizza and feed you
two aspirin.

It was the summer our friends stopped calling you,
sick of your vodka-infused honesty.
It was the summer my girlfriend said kissing me
was too much like trapping herself on flypaper.

We sat in the kitchen, stared into twin coffee cup reflections.
The chairs all too broken to sit in.

INHERITANCE

I have double vision.
I have two school bus stops.
Two Christmas stockings.
Two spots at two dinner tables.

He walked into my band concert
with a woman on either side of him,
but I don't have two moms.
He had a wife. He has a wife.
He has women.

Music seeps out from under his bedroom door.
He grabs each instrument he owns
like it's his favorite.
I have one guitar. I marvel at him,
pressing down six strings with just one finger.
I have his hands.

My mother sleeps in a half-empty bed,
bakes spiced bread to suffocate the smell
of the unfamiliar sweet he dragged home.
I have my mother's eyes. I have his hands
to cover them with. Maybe
I'll have women.

I have two sisters.
He has two daughters.
We teach by example. They will learn
to be someone's women.

He has a room full of guitars.
Now I have two. I forget about the second
because of how much I love the first,
but it will always be there, waiting for me to play.

When I do,
I hold it by the neck
with his hands.

BITCH

Someone is speaking as they always do.
Radio hits boast of a conquest.
A man insults another man
by calling him the worst thing.

Nobody notices the way the word
races off, searching for a neck
to wrap around—this endless

running with scissors.
This is someone's daughter.

Birthday Girl

My little sister has a chocolate-cake beard and my mom chases her
with napkin hands. Somehow I am one whole number bigger
than I was yesterday. I sit in the corner and watch the other girls
dance—my feet don't understand how to carry me. My dress, a parachute
I cannot open. Aunt Amy took the Magician's bunny
and now he's crying because she's pretending to hurt it,
only she's pretending too well and it's not moving anymore.
Mom says *Let's Open Presents.* I know they should be for me
but that's not my name on the wrapping. Happy Birthday to You.
Happy Birthday Dear—That's not my name! Another boy
steals my toy and starts playing with it. I shriek like a teapot.
Dad stops me, says *This is your party. It's your birthday!*
Nothing feels right. My dress is a ribbon uncurling
or I'm ripping it off. I can't tell. The room laughs
like a popcorn bag in the microwave. I am drowning
the new Barbies that shouldn't belong to me.
I grab the cake knife, start chopping
at my pigtails or maybe I'm just pretending.
I'm not actually moving.
I wonder how many
whole numbers bigger
I have to grow to make
this celebration
stop.

THOUGHTFUL ME RUNS INTO ASSHOLE ME AT THE BANK

The bank teller smiles at him and asks about his day.
He grunts at her, corners of his mouth
dragging along the tiled floor, eyes rolling away.

In line, his pocket begins ringing. He pulls out a phone
and shoves it into my hands as if it were a grenade.
He's ignoring the call. I wanted to answer it.

He is there to give me rent.
It is always in all pennies. He watches me
carry it out, stumbling under the weight.

He threatens to move out every month.
You'll miss me when I'm gone.
Can't ever pack a suitcase, though.

If he left, I fear I'd stumble into his room
drunk on annoyance, wake up
and start burning the pancakes on purpose.

LAMPROCAPNOS SPECTABILIS

In the rebirth of spring
my father shows me how to layer mulch,
the difference between annuals
and perennials—which flowers
come back.

His garden wraps around
the house like a wedding ring.
Vines peer through the windows
as my mother folds shirts, the other woman's
perfume staining her hands.
My father is carving her name
into the leg of each chair.

When he leaves, my mother
keeps weeding his bed of flowers.
Each invader plucked out of the earth,
hairs ripping from his beard.

WAITING

Nobody told her Dad was picking me up from school.
At her house, she left Christmas cookies,
Santa's sugar jacket a half-inch thick.
A note that read:

Thought you might like a treat after school.
Please call when you get home.
Love, Mom.

She drilled a pencil into her desk, staring at the receiver.
A child with my jacket skipped into a stranger's van.
She felt something tugging on her sweater,
but found it was her own hand.

PHOTOGRAPH: MY FIRST DAY OF PRESCHOOL

My elastic-waistband pants pulled up to my armpits.
My hair—a cut better suited for a PTA President Mom—
a cut that makes you certain my name is Pat,
and I love the Green Bay Packers and cheap vodka.

My smile—a goofy display of dentist-approved baby teeth,
grape-juice stains at the corners.
Before ever entering the school building, it promises that I will
raise my hand with an answer before the teacher asks
the question. This tongue was built to tattle.

This is my game day.
Finally, a stadium I was built for.

ACROSTIC FOR CLEVELAND

Midway through the day we spent hiding under a fort of hotel room blankets, eating fortune cookies, dedicating The Cure lyrics to each other, and giggling like two children clutching the same secret, I fell in love with you as you were right then—pajamas, morning breath. I started hiding your name everywhere, left it on the mirror, carried it home under my tongue.

Madison, Wisconsin

"The United States is really just New York and LA. Nothing else matters."
—My Environmental Lit Professor

There are cows on parade at the state capitol once a month during Farmer's Market Season, but any Saturday of the summer you can spot a gathering of lesbians. In my high school, there were queer kids everywhere and the Young Republicans never had a yearbook photo—for security reasons. The first thing I learned, once I had my driver's license, was how to safely skid across four lanes of icy traffic. And how to not hit deer.

When I told my parents I was a vegetarian, they asked what I was going to do during the World's Largest Bratwurst Festival. I worry that if I ever became a vegan, I'd find a pile of cheese curds protesting in my bed.

I have heard every joke about living in the Midwest. Been asked if I own a farm, why my vowels draw out like a weed being pulled from a garden. I am too city for the farm kids, too country for cosmopolitan snobs.

Yes, the government took over our corn and we now grow fields of diet soda. Yes, I am prone to thinking that winter boots or sports sandals are appropriate footwear for any occasion. But if you look closely behind the punch lines, there are rolling hills and miles of woods waiting to show you why we stay.

At night in Madison, the moon bends down to skate the surface of Lake Monona. The skyline is not big, but shines like an old friend's smile. Biking through the country, you can watch a pulsing orchestra of fireflies. On the other side of the state, the river bends like a violin bow too great for our ears. This is music you cannot find in a metropolis.

Soon, I'll be the scarecrow in Union Square. New York is the fancy new suit perched on my shoulders, but Madison is the mud caked to the bottom of my feet, the home always dragging from my heels.

WHITE ME TALKS TO AN EMPTY ROOM ABOUT HIS SKIN

Once I wrote a poem where the narrator was a black man. I'm the writer, not the narrator. I don't remember how old I was when I learned that I was white. I never knew something so normal needed a name. I looked the same as every other kid at my school until a new family moved in—a single drop of dye spilling into a suburban pool of water. Once I was stopped by a cop for riding my bike right through a red light across four lanes of traffic at three in the morning and walked away with no ticket. It wasn't about race. In the poem I don't make him sound black. I don't shadow him in sloppy drawl or urban grime. I studied racism in my college classroom while texting beneath the table. I wore a flannel shirt that cost a week's worth of groceries and looked like I pulled it out of a garbage disposal. I wore my hood up in class and nobody told me to take it off. I mentored a group of inner-city youth. I couldn't try the red beans and rice because they cook with pork and I'm a vegetarian. It wasn't about race. I didn't even want to impersonate a black man, but I wanted to write the poem. It was my duty to write the poem. Once I got offered a part-time job—and then another, and then another. Bosses liked the big words I used. Integral. Holistic. Experiential. I have been told that my blue eyes are easy to talk to. A stranger once handed me her baby at a bus stop while she rummaged through her bag because I had a familiar smile. It wasn't about race. The other guy in the poetry workshop with pale skin and an ally of a pen told me my poem was important and everyone should hear me read it. I have always known I was important.

III.

SEVEN-YEAR-OLD ME TAKES SEVENTY-YEAR-OLD ME TO THE PLAYGROUND

The old man is so boring.
He just wants to sit and read.
I want to play on the swings
but there's nobody to push me.

He won't look at me.
I shot a spitball and it whizzed
past his ear, but he just coughed
into his sleeve and kept scowling.
The birds are going to confuse him
for a statue if he doesn't smile soon.

Maybe I'll tell a joke.
If I'm funny enough I can make him laugh.
If I can make him laugh I'll know
I did a good job.
If he stays sad, then I'll sit in the sand
and trace around my feet and try
to be a big boy who doesn't cry.

Kids are building sandcastles with their friends.
The old man doesn't like the giggles.
He glares at them like they're bad puppies.
All anything ever does is bother him.

I want to play the game with him.
I stare at a cloud until it's not fluffy enough.
I don't smile for one hundred years.

ANNA

Mom backed the car down the driveway,
balanced her coffee, told Caroline for the third time
to keep her seatbelt on,

and realized that she only had two kids with her,
not three.

We rushed back to the front door,
Caroline and I laughing, Mom red as a scraped knee.
There, framed by the scrawny window, was Anna:

tears rushing down to her
light-up Barbie sneakers. She was always quiet,
soft as the wind petting our grassy yard.

Seven years later,
she took up Irish Step Dance—
the loudest hobby my family had ever endured.

When she practiced, it sounded like a thunderstorm
crashing through the basement. She could not walk down the halls—
she jigged, rattling the dinner glasses.

My first night away at college,
I could still hear her heels clicking,
too loud to leave behind.

OXFORD COMMA THE CAT TALKS BACK
after Megan Falley

Jesus Christ, Miles. Could you have given me a snobbier name?
Imagine you were named after a punctuation mark:
everyone too busy laughing to bend down to pet you.
I am more than a pause, you bastard. I am an exquisite cuddler.
I'm the best at sitting right between you and the words of a book,
a delicate reminder of what really matters.
Without me, who would lick the peanut butter
from your oatmeal bowls before you were finished?

I don't understand why I'm living in your mom's house now.
Sure, she buys me the tastier food
from that TV commercial with the pretty tinkling bell noises,
and yeah, those stairs I get to climb up and down
really are doing great things for my figure.

Okay, so you were headed off for a grand adventure—
mountains and skyscrapers and a new love—human things.
My adventure will always be sitting in a windowsill,
keeping watch on these pesky birds.
I cannot understand why you need to leave.
Cats feel attached to place. I am happy so long as I'm home.

It's not just that you go, Miles. It's that you refuse to believe it matters.
I've watched you dart from place to place as if you do not leave footprints,
a breeze running through everyone's hair.
You have convinced yourself that you are an empty
soda can rolling down the sidewalk, somebody's leftovers,
but you are my favorite plaything.
You're even better than the shiny fish on the pink string
I got too excited about and chewed through.

You know, Miles. Cats never forget.
I'll remember you when you're ninety and I'm still a young seven
(I'll be on my fifth or sixth life, but we both know I'll stay fresh.)
And I guess when you come home you can share the couch with me.
This will always be your home,
no matter how many cities unroll like a tail behind you.

Silly human boy. Don't you know you're the laser I am always chasing after?
I notice when the red light disappears, and am forever waiting
for it to come back.

CHRISTINA

She is the only seventeen year old
I've ever heard say *Vagina*
without spilling into giggles
like a lunch tray into a lap.

For her, the word is mechanics,
a sterile doctor's office,
a police officer, shuffling though paperwork.
Her crying father.

Most times, she says it anesthetically.
But once in a while
I hear her bark it,
state it with the authority
of someone who owns
what they were so afraid
she'd lost forever.

THE WRITER

Every morning while we are eating breakfast a car smashes through the front window, tires shredding up the carpet like a steel tiger. Roaring past me, it claws for her. She is pinned to the wall by the hood. We know it is coming. My job is to sit still and wait for it to vanish. I can't even sweep up the shards or filter the smoke out the dining room. My job is to wash the dishes while she twists her way out.

The first time, it was messy—bruises down her spine, red blooming across her abdomen. Sitting in the bath together, I told her how much it hurt to watch. So look away, she said. I lost the urge to run months ago. It happens whether or not I am there to witness it.

She pens each day however she likes—picks the make and model of the car, the speed at which it storms into her. Once, the car moved so slowly I swear it was trying to nuzzle into her lap. Another time, it zoomed so fast I didn't even know to break the conversation until I heard her scream. She cleans the wreckage herself, gets into bed without complaint. The limp disappeared months ago—now she doesn't even seem sore.

There is no version of the story where I rip off the engineer's hands so he can't build the car, no way to set back every clock so she never thinks it's time to eat. There is no version where I leap in front of her and save her from impact—my job is to trust that she knows the escape route of each telling.

Sometimes I sit alone in the kitchen and listen for the squealing tires, thinking if I wish hard enough the engine will roar for me instead. It is always silent as a blank page. I cannot own this crash. I cannot will myself into understanding. I can be there when the wheels reverse across the rubble. When the headlights disappear from the kitchen. When she finally writes the beast back out the window.

On Loving a Survivor

I was a trunk of hibernating bullhorns,
a tambourine hanging lifeless in a glass case.

You asked me
for the loudest opposite of neutral,
to be a marching band in a library.
Whether holding flowers or banners—
to show up to the fight.

I am peeling down to my best self,
exhaling my telephone static.
There is no space for silence.
This is the breath before a yell,
the promise of sound.

LETTER TO MY VAGINA

You can be sort of a diva.
The way you periodically
announce your presence—
rolling out your own red carpet.
You are the boozed-up celebrity flashing the audience.
My boxer-briefs: the black censor strip.

You are what makes me newsworthy.
People ask about you,
hunting for what sort of monster
I am naked.

I watched women recoil at the sight of you.
A lover, after kissing you for the first time,
ignored us for weeks.

What did you say to her?

I am told to hide you
like an embarrassing family secret,
ballooning womb beneath a button-down,
the dinner place left off the table.

Even if I explain that we are stuck together,
you are always the rotten surprise:
a lipstick stain hidden by a necktie.

People cannot understand that we're happy
in our body, a dysfunctional family
in a home always on fire. To hate you
would be like taking a power drill to my eardrum,
steak-knifing my right hand.

But I'm scared your loud mouth will get us both in trouble.
I'm scared no woman will want you enough to stay.

FIRST SHOWER

The bathroom door is pushed back,
towels knocked to the ground.

The sink perks up, has no idea
that we have pulled and grabbed each other

all the way across your house—your pants in the living room,
my shirt tossed above the coffee maker—as if we could grind

ourselves into the same sweating dust. Your razor notices
that my body is a murky reflection of yours.

The soap certain that nobody wants to hold a man
who curves same as his lover.

I keep my underwear on.
So do you.

We are both learning to trust, my stomach inching towards yours,
drawn to the warmth of diving into you.

I brush the water from your eyelashes,
You massage my hair,

looking only at my face, waiting for me
to guide your hands down my sides.

Nothing expected you to want all of me,
but here we are now, your underwear

in a pile in the corner of the shower.
Right beside mine.

AUGUST
after Cristin O'Keefe-Aptowicz

The hummus that looked too much like cat vomit,
the half-iced tea, half-lemonade I nervously knocked
into your plate, now a sludge sea with tiny falafel islands.
How the peanut butter slid off my bagel,
blanketed my mouth, cemented my tongue.
The macaroni and cheese we coated in garlic powder,
my bad breath too shy to curl into yours, how it knotted itself
around the noodles instead. Curry for breakfast,
cupcakes for dinner, frosting trimming our wine glasses.
How for dessert we dressed a bucket of cherry tomatoes
under a veil of sea salt—kissed them
into our mouths. And finally, how we feasted.
How we placed every ingredient on the counter
before realizing how tired we were. Ate microwaved
veggie burgers on the couch instead.
How delicious they were.
How it was not what we had planned,
and how we savored every bite.

BIOLOGY

The day I saw two boys aiming a magnifying glass
to the asphalt and did not understand why,

my father drove me home, took out his pocket knife—
its brilliant red casing and infinite tools—
pulled out the tiny magnifying glass
and taught me how to make the sidewalk smoke.

My father is not a gun man; he is a science man.
I grew up with a greenhouse in my kitchen, cages
full of birds in the basement. My father taught me
science is the foundation of everything.

My pocket knife was baby blue, Girl Scouts of America
engraved on its side. It had two blades, both dull
as a toy house's plastic utensils.
My father gifted it to me before a big camping trip—
to carve soap.

When I told my father I was a boy,
he did not say I was wrong.
But it was as if I had insisted
the earth was as flat
as my bound chest.

How could I unexplain the fundamental?

He looked at me, as if his eyes
could magnify the disobedient part of me
and smoke it out of my system: *It's just,
well, doesn't biology trump everything else?*

THE MAN I AM TRIES TO TAKE THE GIRL I WAS THROUGH AIRPORT SECURITY

If you pat me down, you will find her.
I carry her with me wherever I go—
she is the opposite of a pocket-knife,
a plea to be soft and open.

I wish you could confiscate her,
but without her I have no baby pictures,
no first word, no tenth birthday party.

Yes, that is her name on the license.
Sometimes I worry she'll try to kidnap
our body, but she is thirteen and scared
and will only ever be thirteen and scared.

Don't let that security agent touch her.
Can't you see her shaking?
As long as she's with me, she is not dangerous.
I am the one who taught her not to attack the body,
ripped the scissors from her fists.

When strange hands come towards us,
I promise her that I will be the loud one,
that she can stay silent. But under your x-ray machine,
it is just her. A female agent frisks the body—her body.
Here I disappear.

While Getting My Blood Drawn at the Trans Health Clinic

I tell the Blood Technician,
No, I will not completely pass out,
but I will come close.
She just squirms in her latex gloves and says,
But I'm a professional
not knowing that I am a professional too.

A professional weenie.

She doesn't need me to remove
my manliest, most rugged flannel,
but now my cold sweat is sliding
down the back of my neck and soaking the collar,
and I do not feel like my manliest, most rugged self.

Be like a tiger, not a cat,
She says as she pulls a rubber band around my arm,
promises I won't even notice the needle inside me.

But the second the needle is inside me,
I FUCKING NOTICE.

As the color falls off my face, I imagine my beard—
how I will scratch against my love's smile.
My father hugs me for the first time in months—
searching for his child in my sharpened cheeks.
I hear myself calling my sisters—
it takes them a moment to recognize my voice.
We laugh at its cracks and dives.

When the last vial is filled,
the technician collects her concern,
hands me a cup of lukewarm water,
and asks how I feel.

Ready, I say.
I'm ready.

Acknowledgements

These poems appeared first in the following publications:

The Bakery – "The First Day of Spring" "The Writer"

Radius – "Bitch" "Christina" "The White Me Talks to an Empty Room About His Skin"

Vinyl – "Inheritance"

IndieFeed Performance Poetry Podcast – "We Eat an Apple in My Bed"

THANK YOU

To my parents—I can only assume I was not an easy child to raise. Praise every higher power that we all survived the middle school years. Thank you for always trying your hardest to understand. I have never felt unloved.

To Anna and Caroline—nobody will ever understand the world the way the three of us do. We are family forever. I love you.

To Megan—you're the shit and I'm knee-deep in it. Thank you for always pushing me to see the best in myself. For pushing me right into this book. It wouldn't have happened without you. There is no better teammate, no brighter love.

To Mateo—I'm so glad you joined Slam Poetry Club and dragged me along during 12th grade lunch. It changed my life.

To Sean—you kicked my ass when I needed it desperately. Thank you for the curt way you express your confidence in my work. You invited me to have fun with my poems, to laugh about my stupid mistakes.

To Ms. Hyzer, Mr. Howe, and Josh Healey—You three are the first people who taught me to trust myself as a writer. Taught me that trusting myself never means not editing. Thank you for having faith in my work. (Ms. Hyzer—look! I finally stopped ignoring your advice!)

To all the HECUA staff—you absolutely turned my world upside down, and I will never know how to thank you. Without my time with you, I wouldn't have dared to dream up these poems.

To Derrick and the Write Bloody Family—Thank you for the opportunity, the invitation to the party.

About the Author

Miles Walser is a graduate of the University of Minnesota with a Bachelor of Individualized Studies in English, Social Justice, and Youth Studies. In 2010 he represented the U of M at the College Unions Poetry Slam Invitational where his team placed 3rd in the nation and he was named Best Male Poet. He has also represented Minneapolis, Minnesota and Madison, Wisconsin at the adult national level in poetry slam, and appeared on Group Piece Final Stage with the former team. In 2012 he won the award for Best Poem by a Male Poet at the Wade-Lewis Poetry Slam Invitational. His work has appeared in literary journals *The Legendary, Used Furniture Review, Radius,* and *The Bakery* as well as the audio podcast *IndieFeed.* He currently lives in Brooklyn with his curmudgeonly cat.

IF YOU LIKE MILES WALSER, MILES WALSER LIKES...

Racing Hummingbirds
Jeanann Verlee

Rise of the Trust Fall
Mindy Nettifee

After the Witch Hunt
Megan Falley

The New Clean
Jon Sands

Reasons to Leave the Slaughter
Ben Clark

Write Bloody Publishing distributes and promotes great books of fiction, poetry and art every year. We are an independent press dedicated to quality literature and book design, with an office in Austin, TX.

Our employees are authors and artists so we call ourselves a family. Our design team comes from all over America: modern painters, photographers and rock album designers create book covers we're proud to be judged by.

We publish and promote 8-12 tour-savvy authors per year. We are grass-roots, D.I.Y., bootstrap believers. Pull up a good book and join the family. Support independent authors, artists and presses.

**Want to know more about Write Bloody books, authors and events?
Join our maling list at**

www.writebloody.com

WRITE BLOODY BOOKS

1,000 Black Umbrellas — Daniel McGinn

38 Bar Blues — C.R. Avery

After the Witch Hunt — Megan Falley

Aim for the Head, Zombie Anthology — Rob Sturma, Editor

American Buckeye — Shappy Seasholtz

Amulet — Jason Bayani

Animal Ballistics — Sarah Morgan

Any Psalm You Want — Khary Jackson

Birthday Girl with Possum — Brendan Constantine

The Bones Below — Sierra deMulder

Born in the Year of the Butterfly Knife — Derrick C. Brown

Bring Down the Chandeliers — Tara Hardy

Ceremony for the Choking Ghost — Karen Finneyfrock

City of Insomnia — Victor D. Infante

The Constant Velocity of Trains — Lea C. Deschenes

Courage: Daring Poems for Gutsy Girls — Karen Finneyfrock, Mindy Nettifee & Rachel McKibbens, Editors

Dear Future Boyfriend — Cristin O'Keefe Aptowicz

Don't Smell the Floss — Matty Byloos

Drunks and Other Poems of Recovery — Jack McCarthy

The Elephant Engine High Dive Revival anthology

Everything is Everything — Cristin O'Keefe Aptowicz

The Feather Room — Anis Mojgani

Gentleman Practice — Buddy Wakefield

Glitter in the Blood: A Guide to Braver Writing — Mindy Nettifee

Good Grief — Stevie Smith

The Good Things About America — Derrick Brown and Kevin Staniec, Editors

Great Balls of Flowers — Steve Abee

Hot Teen Slut — Cristin O'Keefe Aptowicz

Henhouse: The International Book for Chickens & Their Lovers — Buddy Wakefield

How to Seduce a White Boy in Ten Easy Steps — Laura Yes Yes

I Love Science! — Shanny Jean Maney

I Love You is Back — Derrick C. Brown

In Search of Midnight — Mike McGee

Junkyard Ghost Revival anthology

Knocking at the Door — Lisa Sisler and Lea C. Deschenes, Editors

The Last Time as We Are — Taylor Mali

Learn Then Burn — Tim Stafford and Derrick C. Brown, Editors

Learn Then Burn Teacher's Manual — Tim Stafford and Molly Meacham, Editors

Live For A Living — Buddy Wakefield

Love in a Time of Robot Apocalypse — David Perez

The Madness Vase — Andrea Gibson

Miles of Hallelujah — Rob "Ratpack Slim" Sturma

The New Clean — Jon Sands

New Shoes On A Dead Horse — Sierra deMulder

News Clips & Ego Trips: The Best of Next Magazine — G. Murray Thomas, Editor

No More Poems About the Moon — Michael Roberts

Oh, Terrible Youth — Cristin O'Keefe Aptowicz

Over the Anvil We Stretch — Anis Mojgani

Pole Dancing to Gospel Hymns — Andrea Gibson

Racing Hummingbirds — Jeanann Verlee

Reasons to Leave the Slaughter — Ben Clark

Rise of the Trust Fall — Mindy Nettifee

Scandalabra — Derrick C. Brown

Slow Dance With Sasquatch — Jeremy Radin

The Smell of Good Mud — Lauren Zuniga

Songs from Under the River — Anis Mojgani

Spiking the Sucker Punch — Robbie Q. Telfer

Strange Light — Derrick C. Brown

Sunset at the Temple of Olives — Paul Suntup

These Are The Breaks — Idris Goodwin

Time Bomb Snooze Alarm — Bucky Sinister

Uncontrolled Experiments in Freedom — Brian S. Ellis

The Undisputed Greatest Writer of All Time — Beau Sia

What Learning Leaves — Taylor Mali

What the Night Demands — Miles Walser

Who Farted Wrong? Illustrated Weight Loss for the Mind — Syd Butler

Workin Mime to Five — Dick Richards

Working Class Represent — Cristin O'Keefe Aptowicz

Write About An Empty Birdcage — Elaina Ellis

Yesterday Won't Goodbye — Brian S. Ellis

CPSIA information can be obtained at www.ICGtesting.com
Printed in the USA
BVOW01s2150060414

349794BV00002BA/8/P

9 781938 912160